THE MILITARY HISTORY OF WORLD WAR II
Volume 10

ASIATIC LAND BATTLES:
THE ALLIED VICTORIES
IN CHINA AND BURMA

The Military History of World War II: Volume 10

ASIATIC LAND BATTLES: ALLIED VICTORIES IN CHINA AND BURMA

by Trevor Nevitt Dupuy
COL., U.S. ARMY, RET.

FRANKLIN WATTS, INC.
575 Lexington Avenue • New York 22

Library of Congress Catalog Card Number: 62-7382
Copyright © 1963 by Franklin Watts, Inc.
Printed in the United States of America

1   2   3   4   5   6   7

Contents

Poorly equipped Chinese soldiers barricade themselves behind sandbag earthworks and fire away with their lone machine gun during the Chinese defense of Chapei.

Early Land Battles in Asia

"The China Incident"

WORLD WAR II began in Asia on July 7, 1937, when Japanese troops attacked Chinese soldiers at the Marco Polo Bridge, near Peking in north China. This was the first move of a carefully calculated plan of conquest by which the Japanese intended to establish what they called the "Greater East Asia Co-Prosperity Sphere." What they really meant by these high-sounding words was the expansion of a strengthened Japanese Empire to include China and other lands of eastern and southeastern Asia.

This was not the first military clash which had taken place between China and Japan. The Japanese had long been preparing for this war of conquest by preliminary wars and campaigns which began with the Sino-Japanese War of 1894-95 and the Russo-Japanese War of 1904-5. These preliminary operations resulted in Japanese annexation of the little kingdom of Korea in 1910, and in their occupation of the great Chinese province of Manchuria in 1931. Korea and Manchuria were the bases from which the Japanese, with their attack on the Marco Polo Bridge, launched their invasion of China in July, 1937. Japan pretended that she was merely restoring peace and order in China, which, she claimed, was unable to govern itself properly. So, instead of admitting that this was a full-scale war of conquest, she called her operations simply "The China Incident."

But it was obvious to the rest of the world that the real reason for Japanese invasion had been to prevent China from growing strong and prosperous under the able leadership of President Chiang Kai-shek. China had long been disturbed by internal disorders, but in the 1920's and 1930's, Chiang — first as a military general, and later as a

1

Japanese guns fire on the walled city of Wanping, southwest of Peiping.

political leader — had brought peace and unity to his country. And so in 1937, despite the much greater military and industrial strength of Japan, the Chinese people rallied to Chiang's leadership to defend their nation against this shameless Japanese aggression.

In the following years of the war Japan was able to conquer most of northern and eastern China. But in the fall of 1941, Chiang and the brave Chinese people were still resisting vigorously. The Japanese held all of China's important seaports and had cut off most of the supply of weapons and other equipment from other countries which the Chinese needed in order to continue the war. But Chiang had moved his capital westward to the city of Chungking, which was located behind difficult mountain ranges. His armies were still obtaining a trickle of American Lend-Lease supplies over the Burma Road. Even the efficient Japanese army was baffled by continual harassment from Chinese guerrilla fighters, and by the way the Chinese peasants carried out Chiang's "scorched earth" policy, destroying crops and villages and railroads in front of every Japanese advance.

Japanese infantrymen crawl through barbed wire entanglements erected to protect Hankow.

WIDE WORLD PHOTO

Japanese troops carry their guns up the mountain to attack Chinese positions.

WIDE WORLD PHOTO

Southeast Asia and the Pacific

THE JAPANESE finally decided that it was too costly to try to fight their way into the vast, mountainous, roadless regions of western China, while at the same time trying to keep control of the hostile population in occupied China. They therefore shifted their attention to the other regions of their planned "Greater East Asia Co-Prosperity Sphere." Instead of continuing their offensives in China, they had decided to conquer the rich regions of Southeast Asia. This would not only greatly increase Japan's wealth and strength, it would cut off China's Burma Road supply line and soon make it easier for the Japanese to defeat the stubborn Chinese people and their army.

The Japanese conquest of Southeast Asia began in early December, 1941. To prevent the United States from interfering, the Japanese navy started this new phase of World War II with a crippling surprise attack on the American fleet at Pearl Harbor, in Hawaii.

The Japanese plans had been thorough and complete. In their initial offensives in December, 1941, and on into the early months of

4

1942, they had been even more successful than they had expected to be. In the Pacific, Japanese forces had conquered the Philippine Islands, the Netherlands East Indies, and other islands of the South and Southwest Pacific Ocean; spearheads were now threatening eastern New Guinea and Australia. On the Asiatic mainland the Japanese had occupied Thailand and defeated British troops to conquer Malaya, Singapore, and most of Burma.

"Run Out of Burma"

IN MARCH, 1942, because the Japanese invasion of Burma had threatened China's one link to the outside world, Chiang Kai-shek had sent Chinese troops to help the British defend Burma. Chiang had appointed his chief of staff, American Lieutenant General Joseph W. Stilwell, to command the Chinese troops in Burma. But despite Stilwell's efforts, and those of British Generals Archibald Wavell,

A Chinese crew stand ready to fire their camouflaged gun.

WIDE WORLD PHOTO

Harold Alexander, and William Slim, the Japanese invaders quickly and decisively defeated Allied forces in Burma. This resulted in the closing of the Burma Road, completing the Japanese blockade of China. It also threatened Britain's control of her great empire in India.

In May, 1942, Stilwell had led a small group of Americans, British, Burmese, and Chinese in a retreat from Burma over the jungled trails of the high mountains separating India from Burma. After he reached India he made a statement that has since become famous:

"We got a hell of a beating. We got run out of Burma and it is humiliating. We ought to find out why it happened, go back and retake it!"

Preparing to "Go Back"

DURING the following months, Stilwell did everything in his power to carry out his promise to "go back and retake" Burma. While building up the strength of the Chinese army, he also made plans to reopen a new land road to China through northern Burma, so as to break the Japanese blockade.

At this time there was only one slender air link between China and her allies. This was a 500-mile aerial route that went over extremely high and rugged mountains between northeastern India and Kunming in southern China. Planes taking this route were subjected not only to the dangers of high mountain peaks and uncertain weather, but also to frequent harassment by Japanese fighter planes based at Myitkyina (pronounced "Mitch'e-nah") in northern Burma. Because they had to fly so high to avoid the mountains and to evade the Japanese planes, American transport plane pilots called this hazardous route "the Hump."

Two Chinese divisions — the 38th and 22nd — had been driven out

A camouflaged C-46 Commando plane flies the "Hump" from India to China.

of Burma into India during the disastrous campaign of 1942. With the approval of Chiang Kai-shek, Stilwell decided to build these divisions up with reinforcements brought back over the Hump in empty supply planes returning from Kunming. These divisions, and another one which Stilwell created in India, became the Chinese-Army-in-India. With this little army, Stilwell planned to move from Ledo, in northeast India, into north Burma during the dry season of 1943-44. The British intended to invade southern and central Burma at this same time, while Chinese troops in Yunnan would attack from southwest China toward Myitkyina.

There were two reasons why Stilwell and British General Wavell decided to wait until the fall of 1943 to begin their reconquest of Burma. In the first place, they knew that it would take about a year to build up strength to prepare their defeated troops for a new offensive operation. Secondly, the climate of Southeast Asia is such that heavy and continuous monsoon rains make military operations almost

7

Chinese coolies, from children to the very old, hand-build the runway and revetments at Kunming, China, so that C-54 transports can keep the supplies coming in.

OFFICIAL U.S. AIR FORCE PHOTO

impossible for half of every year. The rains begin in May and last into October, so the Allies planned to complete their preparations in time to start back into Burma when the dry weather began around November, 1943.

In the meantime, Wavell decided to try to restore the confidence of British troops by two small operations in the coming dry season of 1942-43. In the first of these, one division was to make a limited offensive in the coastal region of southwestern Burma known as the Arakan. The Japanese had very few troops in the Arakan, and because of mountains and lack of roads they would not be able to send in reinforcements easily. But the British advance in the Arakan in December, 1942, was too slow and too cautious. The Japanese sent reinforcements, then counterattacked, and early in 1943 they drove the British back to the Indian frontier.

Soon after this, a brigade of three thousand specially trained British soldiers called "Chindits," under the leadership of Brigadier Orde C. Wingate, made a daring raid deep behind the Japanese lines in central Burma. This raid was more successful than the ill-fated Arakan offensive, and Wingate's Chindits were able to fight their way back to India after causing some damage to the Japanese. But the damage had been less than Wavell or Wingate had hoped for — and the Chindits lost over one thousand men.

The failure in the Arakan and the disappointing results of the Chindit raid caused Wavell to decide that his troops would not be ready for a full-scale invasion of Burma in the fall of 1943. He decided to postpone the invasion for an entire year, until November of 1944, meanwhile raising more troops, and giving them intensive training in India.

Stilwell had never liked the British very much. When he learned that Wavell had decided to postpone his part of the invasion, the American general was disgusted. But he was equally furious with his Chinese allies. At about this time Chiang Kai-shek decided that because of the lack of supplies reaching China over the Hump aerial supply route, Chinese troops in Yunnan would not take part in the proposed offensive in November, 1943.

The entire plan for Allied reconquest of Burma in 1943-44 was now ruined — or so it seemed to most people.

"Kachin Scouts," made up of American and British officers and men, Chinese and jungle-wise Kachin natives, burrow in jungle growth as they take up a position to ambush the enemy in Burma.

WIDE WORLD PHOTO

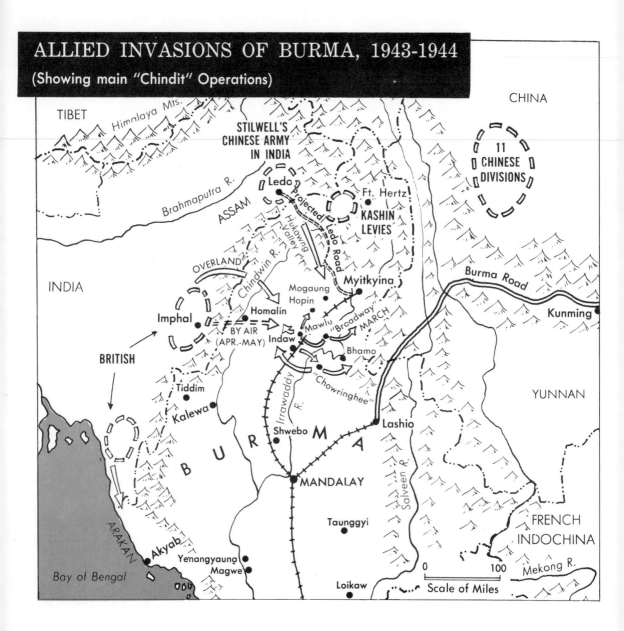

ALLIED INVASIONS OF BURMA, 1943-1944

(Showing main "Chindit" Operations)

CHINA

TIBET

Himalaya Mts.

STILWELL'S
CHINESE ARMY
IN INDIA

Ft. Hertz

11
CHINESE
DIVISIONS

Brahmaputra R.

ASSAM

Ledo

Projected Ledo Road

KASHIN
LEVIES

INDIA

OVERLAND

Hukawng Valley

Chindwin R.

Mogaung
Hopin

Myitkyina

Burma Road

Kunming

Imphal

Homalin

BY AIR
(APR.-MAY)

Indaw

Mawlu

"Broadway"

MARCH

BRITISH

Bhamo

YUNNAN

Tiddim

"Chowringhee"

Irrawaddy R.

Kalewa

Salween R.

B U R M A

Shwebo

Lashio

MANDALAY

Taunggyi

FRENCH
INDOCHINA

ARAKAN

Akyab

Yenangyaung
Magwe

0   100

Mekong R.

Bay of Bengal

Loikaw

Scale of Miles

The Long Road Back to Burma

Into the Hukawng Valley

EVEN THOUGH he felt that he had been let down by the British and the Chinese, Stilwell was determined to carry out his plan for an advance from India. By early November, 1943, the leading regiment of the rebuilt Chinese 38th Division reached Shinbwiyang in the Hukawng Valley of northwestern Burma. Behind the 38th, American engineers were pushing a road from Ledo across the jungled mountains. The 22nd Division was entering the final phase of its training, and would soon follow the 38th into Burma. The situation looked good.

Suddenly the Japanese struck back in the Hukawng Valley. They attacked and surrounded the three battalions of the leading Chinese regiment. Instead of advancing, the Chinese and their American advisers unexpectedly found themselves fighting a desperate defensive battle.

Stilwell rushed to the front to see what was the trouble. Under his inspiring personal leadership the 38th Division began to move. Stilwell exposed himself in the front lines, ignoring snipers, correcting mistakes, and praising good work. The surrounded battalions were rescued and the advance was resumed, though more slowly than the impatient Stilwell liked. But the demands of his other duties forced him to return to his headquarters in New Delhi and Chungking.

The Chinese and "Merrill's Marauders"

LATE IN FEBRUARY of 1944, Stilwell returned to the front, this time accompanied by the first American ground combat unit to arrive in

11

Merrill's Marauders advance against retreating Japanese troops in Burma.

his theater. This was an infantry regiment which is known to history as "Merrill's Marauders," from the name of its commander, Brigadier General Frank D. Merrill.

Although Merrill's regiment had only three thousand men, Stilwell planned to use it to spearhead attacks and to encourage the Chinese to move more quickly. Stilwell understood the psychology of the Chinese soldiers very well, and he knew that they would not want to "lose face" by permitting the Americans to advance faster than they were willing to do.

Stilwell's strategy and psychology proved sound. In early March his Chinese and American troops attacked the Japanese 18th Division near Maingkwan. While the Chinese made a frontal attack against Japanese positions, the Marauders made an encirclement, partly cutting the Japanese lines of communications and inflicting heavy casualties. Only by a rapid withdrawal and skillful delaying actions was Lieutenant General Shinichi Tanaka, commanding the 18th Division, able to save his command from destruction.

The Allied troops pressed rapidly forward. While the main body drove southward behind the retreating 18th Division, Stilwell sent the Marauders and a Chinese regiment to cut a trail through the jungle in order to get behind the Japanese near the tiny village of Shaduzup.

Again the Japanese were decisively defeated, and two of Tanaka's regiments were trapped. Between March 28 and April 1, 1944, Tanaka's men cut their way out of the trap in a desperate battle, but they suffered severe losses and had to abandon much equipment and ammunition. But the Japanese general showed his skill, resourcefulness, and determination by counterattacking, and for a while his troops isolated one of Merrill's battalions in a mountain village southeast of Shaduzup.

During these operations the Chinese and American combat troops

13

Merrill's Marauders on patrol in the jungles of Burma.

had their food, ammunition, and all other supplies delivered to them by air in American transport aircraft flying from bases in northeastern India. Most of the supplies were dropped directly from the planes into jungle clearings immediately behind the frontline units.

Then, unexpectedly, Stilwell and his troops realized that the sources of their supply — and indeed their own existence — were greatly threatened by dramatic developments elsewhere. But before we see how this happened, we must look at other important events that had been taking place on the southern and central fronts.

14

The Second Arakan Campaign

ALTHOUGH the British had decided not to attempt a major invasion of Burma in 1943, they did plan to make another limited offensive in the Arakan. The American-British Combined Chiefs of Staff had recently appointed British Admiral Lord Louis Mountbatten as the Supreme Commander of the newly created Southeast Asia Command. He was now in charge of all Allied troops in India, Burma, and Ceylon. Like Wavell, he wanted British troops to get more confidence in their ability to fight the Japanese in the jungle, and thought this could best be done in the Arakan area. Mountbatten also knew that this limited offensive would keep the enemy from concentrating against Stilwell's invasion in the north.

On November 30, 1943, the three divisions of the British XV Corps advanced toward Akyab. They were soon halted by the Japanese 55th Division, which had fortified a mountain spur extending westward to the sea, blocking the only possible overland approach to

British patrols in Burma, knee-deep in water, hunt for Japanese soldiers in a native village.

WIDE WORLD PHOTO

Allied troops clamber up a typical Arakan hillside during a daylight attack.

Akyab. For two months the British hammered in vain at the powerful defenses. Meanwhile, the new Japanese commander in Burma, Lieutenant General Shozo Kawabe, sent another division to the Arakan.

Suddenly, on February 4, 1944, the Japanese launched a counterattack. They used the same tactics that had been so successful a year earlier: while one division attacked the British front, other troops circled through the jungles to the east, crossing the mountains behind the British flank, and cutting the communications lines of both British frontline divisions.

For several days it seemed that the Second Arakan Campaign would be a repetition of the previous year's disaster in the same area. The Japanese completely surrounded the 7th Indian Division. This time, however, the isolated British units held their ground. Assisted by an emergency air supply, they fought off attacks from all directions. General Slim, now commanding the British Fourteenth Army, rushed reserve divisions to the front. The British counterattacked aggressively.

Suddenly the situation was changed. The Japanese encircling force now found itself surrounded, and by February 20, 1944, it was almost completely wiped out. Only a few Japanese stragglers escaped back to the jungle to rejoin the main Japanese lines.

The XV Corps then resumed its interrupted attacks against the main Japanese defenses. Determinedly the British fought their way through position after position, overcoming fanatic resistance. In late March and early April, the 36th Indian Division broke through the center of the Japanese line. The advance toward Akyab continued — but then the same events that threatened Stilwell's forces forced the British to halt their Arakan offensive.

Lieutenant General Sir William Slim, commander of the British Fourteenth Army.

General Orde Wingate (center) briefs Air Commando Glider pilots just before they take off for the heart of the Burma jungles.

The Second Chindit Raid

IN EARLY MARCH, while the Arakan struggle was still in doubt, and while General Stilwell was advancing southward in the Hukawng Valley, General Wingate and his Chindits suddenly appeared again in north central Burma. They began operating about 100 miles south of Stilwell's front lines, and 200 miles north of Mandalay. This time Wingate commanded an entire division, more than 20,000 men.

The leading Chindit elements had been flown in by gliders. They were to seize jungle clearings in isolated regions deep behind the Japanese lines. Quickly they hacked out landing strips long enough for "Dakotas" (C-47 transport planes) to land. Three brigades were then flown in to these landing strips, while another brigade marched overland from Ledo to join them. The transport planes that flew the Chindits to Burma, and then supported them by air supply, belonged to an American air group commanded by Colonel Philip C. Cochrane.

While several columns of Chindits spread out over the Japanese rear areas to create confusion and to destroy supplies, the main body established a strong defensive position at the town of Mawlu, cutting the railroad line from Mandalay to Myitkyina. Because it was soon strewn with supply parachutes, the British called

C-47 tow-planes and gliders fly over the mountains in Burma.
U.S. AIR FORCE PHOTO

For loading and unloading the "Hump" transports, elephants were found to be faster and more efficient than men. Here an elephant loads 55 gallon drums of gasoline from a truck to a C-46 in India.

U.S. AIR FORCE PHOTO

their position "White City" — the name of an amusement park in London.

Soon after this, on March 25, 1944, Wingate was killed in an airplane crash. He was replaced by Major General W. D. A. Lentaigne. The grieving Chindits continued to carry out Wingate's plans.

At this time, General Kawabe was assembling forces for a full-scale invasion of eastern India. Because of this, and because of the fierce fighting going on in the Arakan and the Hukawng Valley, General Kawabe could not spare any large forces to deal with the Chindit raid. He did, however, scrape up several small units to try to reopen the railroad at Mawlu. These Japanese — some six thousand men — made a number of desperate but unsuccessful attacks against White City.

Early in May, newly arrived Japanese reinforcements were sent from Rangoon to join in the attack against the Chindits at Mawlu. Lentaigne then decided to withdraw his troops from the White City railroad block. At the same time, he sent another brigade further north to a position overlooking the railroad near Hopin. This position the Chindits called "Blackpool."

The Japanese immediately attacked, and for several days a violent battle raged. By this time the British raiders were on the verge of exhaustion and had suffered heavy casualties. As Japanese pressure against Blackpool mounted, the battered Chindits again withdrew, this time to the relative safety of the mountains further west.

Like the first raid, this second Chindit expedition had been a gallant effort, and this time the effort had been a bit more successful. But although the Chindits had inflicted considerable damage on the Japanese, they had not seriously upset Kawabe's plans. The results of the expedition were hardly worth the terrible Chindit losses of over five thousand killed and wounded, with most of the rest put out of action by exhaustion and disease.

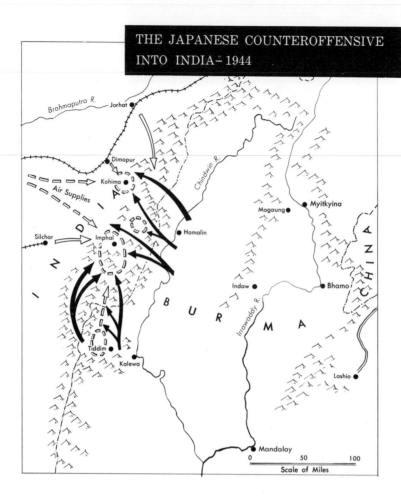

The Japanese Strike Back in Burma and China

The Invasion of India

GENERAL KAWABE had assigned to his Fifteenth Army the mission of inviding eastern India. This army, consisting of three extra-large divisions, comprised nearly 100,000 veteran combat troops. On March 6, 1944, they crossed the Chindwin River on a broad front

22

between Kalewa and Homalin. Two divisions headed for Imphal; the third drove further north toward Kohima. It was this advance that caused the Allies suddenly to stop their offensives in north Burma and the Arakan.

Allied spies and air reconnaissance had provided warning of the Japanese plan to invade India, but the British were completely surprised by the speed of the Japanese advance through the densely jungled mountains. British outposts east of the India-Burma border retreated in confusion. The 17th Indian Division, holding the Chin Hills south of Imphal, was cut off by fast-moving Japanese spearheads. Withdrawing up the Tiddim Road, the division fought its way through repeated Japanese roadblocks, finally reaching Imphal on April 5. They were only one jump ahead of the Japanese main body, which was approaching from the east.

General Slim now set about rectifying his underestimate of Japanese capabilities. The main danger at the moment was that the attackers might seize Dimapur, on the Assam Railway. This would cut off all supplies for the entire Allied central front. It would also stop

Allied Air Commandos, some of them wounded, relax at the edge of a landing strip deep inside Burma.

the flow of supplies to Stilwell's troops and to the Chindits in north Burma. It would also stop all supplies destined for China by way of the Hump airfields.

Though Slim rushed all available reserves to Manipur, by early April the Japanese 15th and 33rd divisions had surrounded the bulk of the British IV Corps' three divisions in Imphal. At the same time the Japanese 31st Division was besieging Kohima. Supplies and food for the British troops, as well as for the 40,000 civilians in the surrounded areas, had to be sent by aircraft.

The Sieges of Imphal and Kohima

WHILE BITTER and confused fighting raged all around Imphal and Kohima, Slim continued to fly in reinforcements to both places. American and British fighter planes and bombers attacked the Japanese and their long supply lines back to Burma. Yet even though they were outnumbered, and though their food and supplies were inadequate, the Japanese continued to attack vigorously. For several weeks the outcome was gravely in doubt.

Slim meanwhile rushed his reserve XXXIII Corps to Dimapur. These troops threw back Japanese spearheads approaching the railroad, then counterattacked southward. On April 20 they broke through the Japanese lines to relieve Kohima. Further British progress, however, was painfully slow. Week after week the struggle continued, as the monsoon rains began to fall. Finally, on June 22, after Imphal had been besieged for eighty days, the IV and XXXIII Corps hacked their way through the last Japanese roadblocks to meet on the Imphal-Kohima Road.

Now it was the Japanese Fifteenth Army that was threatened by disaster. They had expected to capture Allied supplies in Imphal and

Riflemen of the 13th Frontier Force hold a battle-scarred hillside in the Imphal area.

Kohima. They had not foreseen that the British would refuse to retreat and abandon those supplies. Consequently they were short of ammunition and, by the end of June, most of the Japanese frontline units were near starvation. Under the circumstances it was amazing that they were able to fight as well as they did against more numerous, well-equipped, well-fed British troops, supported by unopposed air power.

The beginning of the rains caused a complete breakdown of the inadequate Japanese supply lines. Slowly their tide receded from Imphal. By mid-July the Japanese Fifteenth Army was collapsing, as Slim's troops pursued closely. Starvation and malaria took a fearful toll. By the time the remnants of the three battered Japanese divisions reached the Chindwin Valley in August and September, they had lost over 65,000 dead.

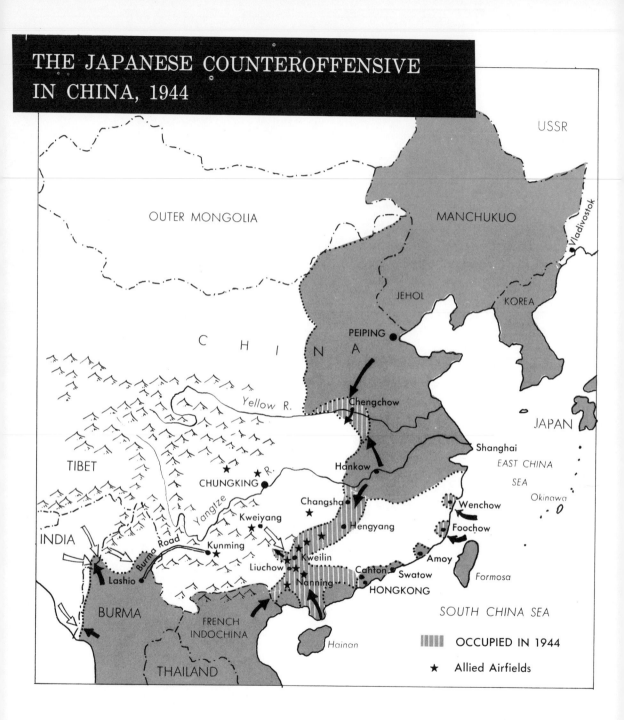

THE JAPANESE COUNTEROFFENSIVE IN CHINA, 1944

USSR

OUTER MONGOLIA

MANCHUKUO

Vladivostok

JEHOL

KOREA

C H I N A

PEIPING

Yellow R.

Chengchow

JAPAN

Shanghai

EAST CHINA SEA

Okinawa

TIBET

CHUNGKING

Hankow

R.

Changsha

Wenchow

Kweiyang

Hengyang

Foochow

Yangtze

INDIA

Burma Road

Kunming

Kweilin

Amoy

Liuchow

Nanning

Canton

Swatow

Formosa

Lashio

HONGKONG

SOUTH CHINA SEA

BURMA

FRENCH INDOCHINA

Hainan

▌▌▌▌ OCCUPIED IN 1944

★ Allied Airfields

THAILAND

Renewed Japanese Offensives in China

DURING 1943, increasing numbers of American transport planes had added greatly to the quantity of supplies being flown over the Hump to China. As a result, the strength of General Chennault's Fourteenth Air Force had grown steadily. By late 1943, the American airmen had gained air superiority over most of China, and their strikes were severely punishing Japanese ground troops. The Japanese decided that the best way to stop this would be to capture the American airfields by ground offensives.

General Stilwell had foreseen that this would be the Japanese reaction to growing American air strength in China. He had fully approved of building up the Fourteenth Air Force, but he felt that this would be dangerous if the Chinese ground strength were not improved with supplies and equipment at the same time. Chennault, however, had insisted that his airmen could stop any Japanese ground offensive simply by intensive bombing and strafing attacks. President Roosevelt and the Joint Chiefs of Staff in Washington had sided with Chennault in the argument between the two generals; Stilwell had been overruled.

On May 27, after preliminary operations to improve their railroad supply lines from northeast China, the Japanese Eleventh Army of 250,000 men began to attack southward from Hankow toward Changsha. At the same time the Japanese Twenty-third Army of 50,000 men struck west from Canton.

At first the Chinese resisted stubbornly. They received very effective support from General Chennault's airmen, but the Japanese continued to drive steadily on, capturing Changsha on June 19.

During the next month, the Japanese met little ground opposition and they advanced about a hundred miles despite constant harass-

Air base installations are keyed back among the limestone buttes at Kweilin, China, making them difficult to strafe. Caves have been utilized for base headquarters, storage, and even hangars for medium bombers.

U.S. AIR FORCE PHOTO

On a cliff overlooking the Salween River, Chinese soldiers wait with automatic rifles for the Japanese to try to cross the river.

WIDE WORLD PHOTO

ment from the Fourteenth Air Force. Then, near Henyang, an important rail junction where the Americans had an air base, the Chinese defense stiffened. At the same time the Fourteenth Air Force fiercely intensified its attacks against the Japanese and their line of communications along the railroad. Nevertheless, the Japanese finally captured the city and the airfield on August 8.

Chinese resistance now broke down almost completely. Chinese troops were short of food and supplies; they were exhausted and dispirited. The Japanese drive continued, although it continued to be hampered by incessant attacks from American airplanes, and was slowed down by the Chinese destruction of roads and railroads.

But the Japanese did not allow these difficulties to stop them. Continuing south and west toward Kweilin they captured one airfield after another. In Washington, President Roosevelt and the Joint Chiefs of Staff grew more and more alarmed by the dismal news from China. The government of Chiang Kai-shek appeared to be about to collapse.

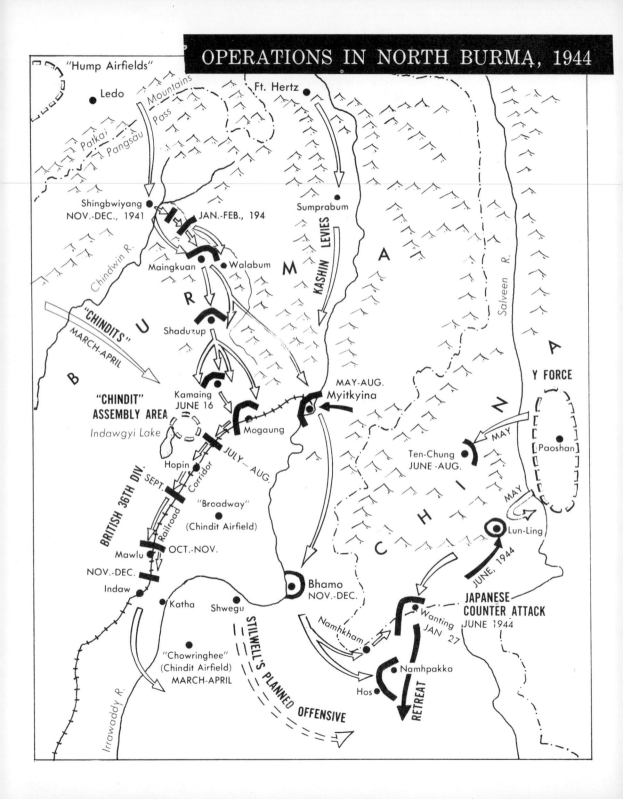

OPERATIONS IN NORTH BURMA, 1944

"Hump Airfields"

Ledo

Patkai

Pangsau

Mountains

Pass

Ft. Hertz

Sumprabum

M   A

Shingbwiyang
NOV.-DEC., 1941

JAN.-FEB., 194

KASHIN LEVIES

Chindwin R.

Maingkuan

Walabum

U   R

M

A

"CHINDITS"

MARCH-APRIL

Shaduzup

Y FORCE

B

"CHINDIT"
ASSEMBLY AREA

Kamaing
JUNE 16

MAY-AUG.
Myitkyina

N

Salween R.

Indawgyi Lake

Mogaung

MAY

JULY — AUG.

Ten-Chung
JUNE-AUG.

Paoshan

Hopin

Corridor

BRITISH 36TH DIV.

SEPT.

Railroad

"Broadway"
(Chindit Airfield)

C   H   I   N

MAY

Lun-Ling

Mawlu

OCT.-NOV.

NOV.-DEC.

Indaw

Katha

Shwegu

Bhamo
NOV.-DEC.

Namhkham

Namkham

Wanting
JAN 27

JUNE, 1944

JAPANESE
COUNTER ATTACK
JUNE 1944

"Chowringhee"
(Chindit Airfield)
MARCH-APRIL

STILWELL'S PLANNED OFFENSIVE

Namhpakka

Hos

RETREAT

Irrawaddy R.

The Struggle for North Burma

Drives to Myitkyina, Kamaing, and Mogaung

BECAUSE of the Japanese Imphal offensive, Stilwell had temporarily halted the advance of his troops in north Burma in late March. Then, in April, confident that Slim would stop the invasion, Stilwell resumed his drive down the Mogaung Valley. But General Tanaka's 18th Division defended stubbornly, and Chinese progress was painfully slow, so Stilwell decided to carry out a plan he had long been thinking about. This was to strike a blow directly at Japanese-held Myitkyina before the beginning of the monsoon.

Myitkyina was the northern terminus of the railroad from Rangoon and Mandalay and it had the only hard-surfaced airfield in north Burma. If the Chinese could capture this field, the Japanese could no longer interfere with the Hump airlift. The transport route from India to China could be shifted south to a more direct course, over lower

A Chinese soldier places a projectile into a heavy 4.2 mortar to shell Japanese positions in northern Burma. Before he could place the projectile, the barrel had to be aimed; another crew member has the task of using the sighting and aiming mechanism.
WIDE WORLD PHOTO

mountains. Also, Stilwell knew that if he could capture Myitkyina, he would be close to breaking the land blockade of China.

In late April and early May the Marauders, now reduced to about fourteen hundred men, accompanied by two Chinese regiments and some British-led, native Kachin Rangers, began a bold but secret advance eastward over the high mountains between the Mogaung and Irrawaddy Valleys. The Japanese had thought these mountains impassable, so they were completely surprised when the Allies suddenly seized the Myitkyina airfield in a dawn attack on May 17.

The next day the Allied troops — by now less than four thousand strong — attacked Myitkyina itself. But although there were only seven hundred Japanese troops in the city at the time, the long and rapid advance had completely exhausted the Americans and Chinese, and their attack was repulsed. Chinese reinforcements were being flown in to the Myitkyina airfield, but the Japanese were also receiving reinforcements from the east bank of the Irrawaddy. So, despite the encouragement and inspiration of Stilwell's personal presence, repeated Allied attacks were unable to break through the stubborn Japanese defenses.

With the first Allied troops to fly into the Myitkyina airstrip came Dr. Gordon Seagrave. To the annoyance of the doctor's Burmese nurses, Stilwell had refused to allow them to accompany him. It was just as well, because Seagrave was at once busy operating on wounded Allied soldiers at the edge of the airfield, ignoring the pouring rain and Japanese bullets whistling around his head.

The Battle of Myitkyina became a drawn-out siege operation of trench warfare. Now Stilwell realized that Merrill's Marauders were collapsing physically under the strain of the long and arduous campaign. Most of them had to be flown back to India, sick and exhausted.

However, the news of the capture of the Myitkyina airfield had

American and Chinese troops in Burma cross an improvised bridge made of planks over gasoline tanks lashed together.

put new life in the Chinese divisions of the Mogaung Valley. Despite the continuing skill and determination of General Tanaka and his 18th Division, the Chinese 38th and 22nd divisions slashed their way southward toward Kamaing and Mogaung. On June 16, Kamaing was captured in a Chinese bayonet assault, the first important Burmese city to be regained by the Allies. Ten days later Mogaung fell to a joint attack by Chinese troops and British Chindits.

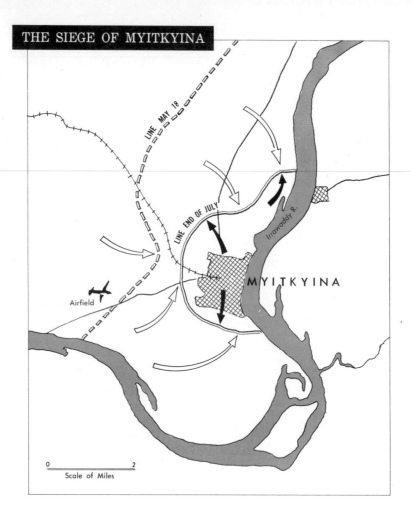

The Siege of Myitkyina

MEANWHILE, at Myitkyina, reinforcements from east of the Irrawaddy had increased the strength of the Japanese garrison to nearly 3,500 men. Allied strength, however, had reached over 30,000, consisting of three Chinese divisions, plus a number of smaller American units. But though they outnumbered the Japanese almost ten-to-one, the Allies were still unable to drive the defenders from their well-entrenched positions. Week after week the discouraging siege dragged on. Now that the Allied positions around Myitkyina were secure Stilwell permitted the Burmese nurses to rejoin Seagrave; at once they did their usual wonderful job of taking care of sick and wounded men.

Finally, late in July, a new series of Allied attacks began to gain some ground. The defenders, now in serious condition from illness, casualties, and short supplies, were driven back into the center of Myitkyina. The Japanese high command, satisfied with the delay that this stubborn defense had imposed upon the Allies, now sent radio orders to the garrison to withdraw. On August 3, the Allies launched a final attack that drove into the city just as the last Japanese crossed the river to safety.

Myitkyina was finally in Allied hands. About 700 Japanese escaped; nearly 3,000 lost their lives in the siege. Allied casualties were more than 5,000.

The outstanding feature of the Siege of Myitkyina was the determination, energy, and skill of the Japanese defenders. They had fought overwhelming numerical odds, and were under constant attack from American fighter and bomber planes. The Americans and Chinese, although they had finally captured the city, did not have

Lieutenant General Joseph W. Stilwell with Generalissimo Chiang K'ai-shek in Burma, April, 1942.

U.S. ARMY PHOTOGRAPH

much to be proud of. Before this fight Americans had been critical of the way in which the British had allowed themselves to be surrounded at Imphal and Kohima by three Japanese divisions. Their experience at Myitkyina made the Americans more respectful of both the British and the Japanese.

Despite the long delay, the final capture of Myitkyina proved the soundness of General Stilwell's strategy. American engineers were rushing the Ledo Road and an oil pipeline across the Hukawng Valley; the land blockade of China was almost broken. The capture of the Myitkyina airfield, which had eliminated Japanese air opposition from north Burma, was already permitting the Hump transport planes to carry much larger loads to China.

The Railroad Corridor Campaign

SOME TIME earlier the Chindits had come under General Stilwell's command. In late June he gave them the mission of protecting his right flank against a possible Japanese counteroffensive up the railroad from Mandalay toward Mogaung. Between Indaw and Mogaung this railroad ran through a long, sheltered valley that the Americans called "the Railroad Corridor."

It soon became obvious to Stilwell, and to British commanders in India, that the Chindits had reached the limit of their endurance just as had Merrill's Marauders at Myitkyina. So they were withdrawn from Burma and replaced by two British infantry brigades of the 36th Indian Division, which were flown to north Burma.

Early in August, under the aggressive leadership of Major General Francis W. Festing, these brigades began to smash their way through determined Japanese resistance southwest of Mogaung. Despite rain and mud, they pushed steadily down the railroad and, on August 28,

Having driven the Japanese from the city of Prome, in Burma, Allied troops go into the city across the railway near the Irrawaddy River.

captured the town of Pinbaw, the objective set by Stilwell. This was the first time in modern military history that a large force had attempted an offensive in Southeast Asia during the height of the monsoon season. The artillery support for this offensive was provided by a Chinese group, under an American commander.*

After capturing Pinbaw, Festing asked Stilwell's permission to patrol southward. Stilwell approved, expecting that for these patrols the

* That American was then-Lt. Col. T. N. Dupuy, author of this book.

British general would use a few squads to scout the Japanese outposts on the railroad south of Pinbaw. Instead, Festing immediately sent two reinforced battalions to push the Japanese out of hastily prepared positions. In a few weeks these aggressive "patrols" advanced the British nearly fifty miles down the railroad. Afraid that they might be cut off, Stilwell ordered Festing not to advance or "patrol" any further. Almost against his will, Stilwell was discovering that there were British soldiers and generals who would fight as aggressively as he did.

Operations in Yunnan

MEANWHILE, in China, the troops in southwestern Yunnan had suddenly come to life. This army, called the "Y-Force," consisted of 72,000 men commanded by Chinese Marshal Wei Li-huang. On May 11 the Y-Force crossed the Salween on a broad front, heading toward the frontier of Burma. Its first objectives were the ancient walled cities of Lun-ling, and Ten-chung. Opposing Wei was the Japanese 56th Division, probably about 15,000 strong. The Japanese, however, were well supplied and equipped, while the Chinese were short of heavy weapons and other essential supplies.

Driving back Japanese outposts, the Chinese gradually surrounded Lun-ling in early June. Then, on June 16, a Japanese counterattack drove them back. Rallying, finally the Chinese halted the smaller pursuing force and reestablished a partial blockade of the city.

At Ten-chung, however, the Chinese were more aggressive. Early in July, aided by excellent close air support from General Chennault's Fourteenth Air Force, Chinese troops began to attack the city. On August 4, they penetrated the walls through a breach made by American fighter bombers. Street by street the Chinese fought on, killing the last defiant Japanese defender on September 15.

While the Chinese were still celebrating this victory, the reinforced Japanese 56th Division counterattacked. The Japanese broke through the troops blockading Lun-ling and drove them back toward the Salween River. But though the Chinese were unable to stop this advance, the Japanese stopped their pursuit because of a new Allied offensive in north Burma.

Stilwell's Last Offensive

AFTER THE CAPTURE of Myitkyina the monsoon caused a lull in the fighting in north Burma, except for the operations of the British 36th Division in the Railroad Corridor. Stilwell reorganized his Chinese and American units and completed plans for a final offensive to clear the Japanese from north Burma. He now had five Chinese divisions plus Festing's 36th Division, and a newly organized American brigade of two regiments. He was opposed by the Japanese Thirty-third Army, which consisted of three divisions.

A Chinese pack artillery outfit moves along a road on the Burma front where mechanized equipment cannot always move.
WIDE WORLD PHOTO

An American sniper in Burma takes up his position in the window of a shell-shattered brick house to watch for the slightest movement that will disclose the position of a Japanese soldier.

The offensive began on October 15, 1944. The 36th Division protected Stilwell's right flank by continuing its drive down the Railroad Corridor. On Stilwell's left the veteran Chinese 38th Division advanced southward along the east bank of the Irrawaddy River toward Bhamo. In the area between these flank drives, four Chinese divisions and the American brigade crossed the Irrawaddy near Shwegu, then swung southeastward across the jungles and mountains toward Lashio. Stilwell intended that this tremendous hammer blow would encircle the entire Japanese Thirty-third Army, which would then be trapped between his Chinese-Army-in-India and the Y-Force in Yunnan.

Suddenly, as the success of this brilliant stroke was within Stilwell's grasp, the advance was halted. Dramatic events in China forced the abandonment of Stilwell's brilliant plan.

End of the China-Burma-India Theater

The Crisis in China

WHILE THE CHINESE divisions in Burma were preparing for the renewed offensive in mid-1944, other Chinese troops in China were still retreating in confusion before the continuing Japanese advance. During the summer, Stilwell continuously shuttled back and forth by air between Burma and China. He arranged for increased Hump deliveries of fuel and ammunition to General Chennault's Fourteenth Air Force, which had used up most of its scarce reserve supplies in fierce air strikes to slow the Japanese advance.

Stilwell also tried to reorganize the main Chinese armies to enable them to resist more successfully. But because of the continuing disagreements between Stilwell and Chiang Kai-shek, the Chinese generalissimo ignored most of the advice he received from the American general.

Key Japanese railroad bridge at Liuchow, China, destroyed by hit-and-run bombers of the 14th Air Force.

PHOTO BY 14TH AIR FORCE

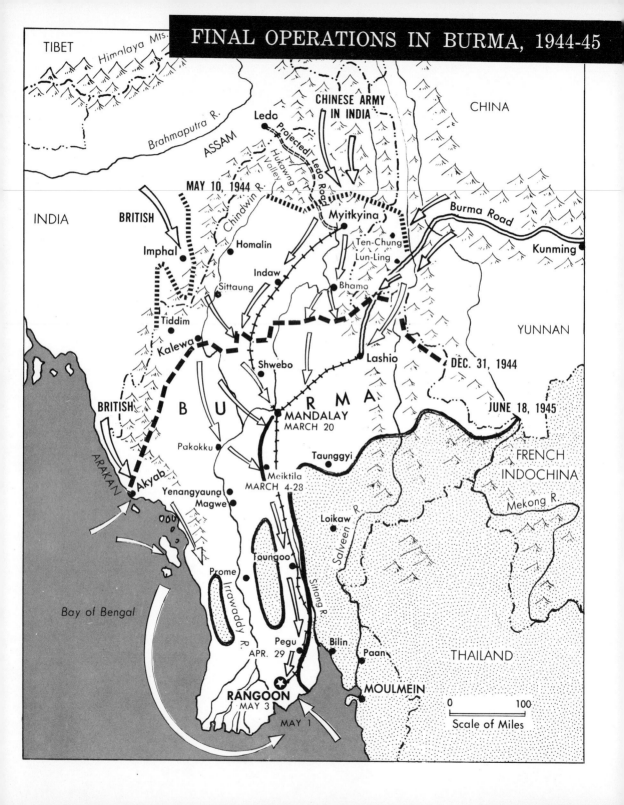

FINAL OPERATIONS IN BURMA, 1944-45

TIBET

Himalaya Mts.

CHINESE ARMY
IN INDIA

CHINA

Brahmaputra R.

ASSAM

Ledo

Projected Ledo Road

INDIA

MAY 10, 1944

BRITISH

Imphal

Homalin

Hukawng Valley

Chindwin R.

Myitkyina

Ten-Chung

Lun-Ling

Burma Road

Kunming

Indaw

Bhamo

Sittaung

Tiddim

Kalewa

Shwebo

Lashio

YUNNAN

DEC. 31, 1944

BRITISH

B   U   R   M   A

Pakokku

MANDALAY
MARCH 20

JUNE 18, 1945

ARAKAN

Akyab

Yenangyaung

Magwe

Meiktila
MARCH 4-28

Taunggyi

FRENCH
INDOCHINA

Mekong R.

Loikaw

Salween R.

Prome

Toungoo

Irrawaddy R.

Sittang R.

Bay of Bengal

Pegu
APR. 29

Bilin

Paan

THAILAND

MAY 1

RANGOON
MAY 3

MOULMEIN

0   100

Scale of Miles

The inability of the Chinese to stop the Japanese land offensive continued to cause great concern in Washington. It looked to the Americans as though China might be forced to surrender to Japan. President Roosevelt at last realized that General Stilwell had been right in insisting upon building up the Chinese army at the same time that Chennault's Fourteenth Air Force was strengthened. The President and the Joint Chiefs of Staff therefore believed that the disastrous situation in China could best be corrected by Stilwell himself. Accordingly, President Roosevelt sent a personal message to Generalissimo Chiang urging him to place Stilwell in full command of all the Chinese armed forces.

Relief of General Stilwell

BY THIS TIME, the differences between Stilwell and Chiang had hardened into personal enmity. Chiang believed that Stilwell had influenced President Roosevelt to recommend his appointment to command Chinese troops. The strong-minded Chinese leader refused, therefore, to agree to President Roosevelt's proposal. Instead, he insisted that Stilwell be recalled from China and be replaced by another, and more diplomatic, American general.

Reluctantly President Roosevelt agreed to Chiang's demand. On October 18, three days after the start of his offensive in Burma, General Stilwell was relieved of his command and recalled to the United States. His China-Burma-India Theater was broken into two parts. Brilliant young Major General Albert C. Wedemeyer was placed in command of the new China Theater and appointed as Chief of Staff to Chiang. Lieutenant General Dan I. Sultan was appointed to command of the India-Burma Theater.

Halting the Japanese Offensive in China

WHILE THIS drama was taking place in the Chinese capital of Chungking, the Japanese continued their offensives against the American air bases in east-central China. On November 11, the Japanese Eleventh Army captured Kweilin. The same day the converging Twenty-third Army seized Liuchow. The fall of these cities, with their important American airfields, was followed soon afterward by the capture of Nanning. This wiped out all of the eastern China air bases of the Fourteenth Air Force. In addition, the Japanese offensives had opened a complete overland line of communications between Korea and Singapore, across all of eastern Asia. This was very important to Japan, since her sea lines of communications were now being badly battered by American naval and air forces operating in the Pacific.

In mid-November, the Japanese began to advance westward toward Kweiyang, Kunming, and Chungking. To stop this new and serious threat, General Wedemeyer requested General Sultan to transfer to him two of the American-trained and -equipped Chinese divisions advancing in Burma. These were promptly shipped north to China by air. Additional reinforcements were gathered from other parts of the front in China. These forces, strongly supported by the Fourteenth Air Force, counterattacked east of Kweiyang. This unexpectedly strong opposition finally stopped the Japanese advance. The immediate danger of complete defeat in China had been averted, but the Japanese threat was far from ended.

Change of Plans in North Burma

THE RECALL of the two Chinese divisions from Burma to China was probably necessary to prevent disaster in China in 1944. However, it

Japanese troops on the move in China.

completely ruined the great offensive which Stilwell had started, and which General Sultan had been continuing in accordance with Stilwell's plan.

Sultan was now forced to set new objectives. He had to abandon the proposed drive to Lashio. This meant that he could no longer hope to encircle the Japanese Thirty-third Army. The reduced Chinese-Army-in-India was given the mission simply of opening and securing the road that stretched east from Bhamo toward the Burma Road. The Japanese, however, were strongly entrenched at Bhamo, and were prepared to hold the high mountains between Bhamo and the Burma Road indefinitely. The land blockade of China could not now be quickly or easily broken.

45

Victory in Burma

Japanese Defensive Plans

IN THE SUMMER of 1944, after the disastrous failure of the Imphal offensive, General Hoyotaro Kimura had been appointed to command Japanese forces in Burma. It was obvious to him that the Allies were preparing to make a full-scale effort to reconquer Burma. He expected them to advance on all fronts as soon as the dry season began late in the year.

Kimura decided that his greatest chance of success would be to let the Allies advance into central Burma, where their supply problems would become difficult. At the same time, Japanese troops would be close to their bases; their supply problems would become easier. In addition to the three divisions opposing Stilwell's advance in the north, Kimura had seven divisions to employ against the expected British offensives. He believed that with these forces he could defeat the Allies once they reached central Burma. He ordered his troops to delay and harass the Allied advance; but they were to avoid an all-out fight until he gave the order to counterattack. He planned to smash the British invaders when they began to cross the Irrawaddy River near Mandalay.

The Importance of Allied Air Supply

THE JAPANESE plan would have been a good one — except for one thing. Kimura did not realize the full importance of Allied air superiority, and the use which the Allies could make of air supply.

The Japanese invasion of India had failed largely because they could not keep up long supply lines through the jungle under the pressure of constant air attack. But the Allies did not depend upon such supply lines to support their troops, or to keep up the advance in the jungle.

Hundreds of Allied transport aircraft based in India brought food, ammunition, and all manner of supplies directly to the frontline troops. If there were no nearby airfields where they could land, the airmen dropped these supplies into rice paddy fields or jungle clearings. Anything that was likely to break was dropped by parachute; all other things were simply dumped out of the planes in what was known as a "free drop."

Thus the Japanese could not really count on a breakdown of Allied lines of communications through the jungle. The only supply line came through air that the Allies controlled completely. And because they had driven Japanese combat planes from the skies, the Allies had no worries about the air strikes against their base areas in India.

Allied troops attack a native hut in a banana grove in Burma.
IMPERIAL WAR MUSEUM, LONDON

The Third Arakan Campaign

THE BRITISH opened their third Arakan Campaign on December 12, 1944. Four divisions of the XV Corps resumed the advance against Akyab. In accordance with Kimura's plan, the Japanese delayed, but did not try to stop the British advance. On January 4, the British occupied Akyab, and the XV Corps began to prepare for an amphibious invasion of south Burma.

Reopening the Land Supply Route to China

THE CHINESE advance toward the Burma Road was held up for over a month by determined and stubborn Japanese resistance at Bhamo. The Chinese 38th Division, however, was equally stubborn. By mid-December, the defenders finally realized that they could not hold out any longer. Rather than surrender, the eight hundred Japanese survivors fought their way out just before dawn on December 15, and soon afterward joined the remainder of the 56th Division in the mountains between Bhamo and Namhkam. About four hundred had been killed in the siege.

Now the Chinese pressed forward aggressively against the 56th Division. At the same time, the Y-Force was advancing down the Burma Road against the right rear of the Japanese division. In the face of these two converging Chinese drives the Japanese withdrew deliberately and skillfully. They did not allow themselves to be trapped; they made the Chinese fight hard for every foot of the ground.

But the Allied pressure was continuous, and on January 27, 1945, the last Japanese troops slipped away southward to permit the Chinese-Army-in-India to meet the Y-Force at Mong Yu, on the

China-Burma border. The Ledo and Burma roads had now been joined.

Meanwhile, General Sultan had ordered a large truck convoy, carrying supplies intended for China, to drive from Ledo to Bhamo. The trucks followed the Chinese troops as they advanced through Namhkam. While they were waiting for the road to be cleared, the truck drivers, and the newspapermen with the convoy, all joined Dr. Seagrave in a party celebrating the recapture of his old hospital at Namhkam.

Then, on January 28, the day after the road was opened, Sultan sent the convoy on into China. These first trucks from the Ledo Road arrived at Kunming on February 4, amidst great rejoicing and celebrations. At the suggestion of Chiang Kai-shek, the combined Ledo and Burma roads were renamed the Stilwell Road, in honor of the man most responsible for breaking the blockade of China.

Although the Chinese and American troops had accomplished their main mission, the war in north Burma was not completely over. During January and February there was bitter fighting along the Burma Road as the Chinese advanced southward toward Lashio. There were

Under a scorching tropical sun, an American mortar crew of the Mars Task Force pounds enemy troop and supply columns.
WIDE WORLD PHOTO

other fierce clashes in the jungle west of the road, as far as the Irra-waddy Valley, where General Festing's 36th Division fought its way to make contact with the left flank of General Slim's advancing Four-teenth Army. But the most important operations in Burma were now taking place farther south and west.

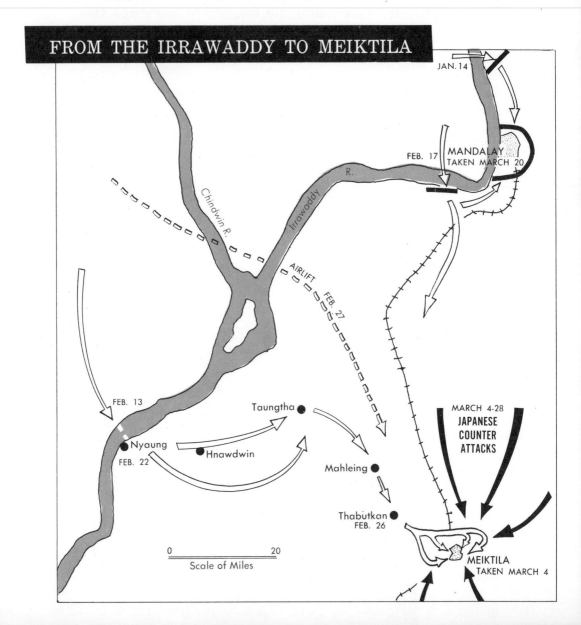

FROM THE IRRAWADDY TO MEIKTILA

JAN. 14

MANDALAY
TAKEN MARCH 20

FEB. 17

Chindwin R.

Irrawaddy R.

AIRLIFT FEB. 27

FEB. 13

Taungtha

FEB. 22
Nyaung
Hnawdwin

MARCH 4-28
JAPANESE
COUNTER
ATTACKS

Mahleing

Thabutkan
FEB. 26

0   20
Scale of Miles

MEIKTILA
TAKEN MARCH 4

British troops cross the Irrawaddy River in their drive to Mandalay.

Across the Irrawaddy

THE LARGEST and most powerful of the Allied forces invading Burma was General Slim's Fourteenth Army. In November, 1944, Slim began his advance toward Mandalay from the Tiddim region of the Chin Hills. Fourteenth Army units crossed the Chindwin River on a broad front between Sittaung and Kalewa. During December, the British spearheads pressed eastward and reached the Irrawaddy River near Shwebo on January 8, 1945.

During the advance toward the Irrawaddy, General Slim realized that the Japanese were not fighting with their usual intensity or

British 3-inch mortar detachments support the Allied advance in Burma.

ferocity. He soon learned from aerial photographs, and from the reports of spies and Allied guerrilla detachments behind the Japanese lines, that General Kimura was concentrating his forces east of the Irrawaddy, around Mandalay.

Slim immediately guessed Kimura's plan for a counterattack near Mandalay, so he secretly shifted most of his IV Corps to the south in order that they would reach the Irrawaddy near Pakokku, about one hundred miles downstream from Mandalay. This movement was made so skillfully that the Japanese did not learn about it.

Meanwhile, many miles to the north of Mandalay, the 19th Indian

Division pretended to be the entire IV Corps. On January 14, this division crossed the Irrawaddy at Kyaukmyaung against strong opposition. At the same time, the XXXIII Corps attracted Japanese attention by making obvious preparations for an attack across the river at the southern outskirts of Mandalay, near Sagaing. The Japanese concentrated troops on the opposite side to oppose the crossing, which began on February 12.

Now, in accordance with General Kimura's plan, and just as Slim expected, the Japanese counterattacked vigorously against the two British bridgeheads, north and south of Mandalay. Despite the intensity of these counterattacks, the British were able to hold on to their footholds east of the river, but were unable to make any advance.

Then, on February 13, the 7th and 17th Indian divisions of the IV Corps crossed the Irrawaddy at Pakokku, without any difficulty. The Japanese paid little attention to this crossing, since they thought it was merely an unimportant diversion. On February 21, British tanks of the 17th Division struck eastward. The infantry of the 7th Division remained to hold a bridgehead at Pagan.

The Battle of Meiktila

THE IRRAWADDY Valley south and east of Mandalay is the broad, flat "dry belt" of Burma, without the thick jungles that cover most other parts of the country. The rice fields were rock hard in the months of February and March, and were ideal maneuvering ground for tanks and trucks. This was why Slim had concentrated most of his armored units in the 17th Indian Division.

There were few Japanese troops to oppose the eastward drive of the British tanks. In six days 17th Division units reached the strategic· towns and airfields of Meiktila and Thazi, on the road and railroad between Mandalay and Rangoon.

British Fourteenth Army troops establish a bridgehead across the Irrawaddy River. In the foreground, wounded men are being brought to a casualty station.

Now, for the first time, Kimura realized that he had been out-maneuvered by Slim. While his attention had been riveted on the bridgeheads near Mandalay, the British tanks had cut the Japanese line of communications with Rangoon.

Immediately large Japanese forces were detached from the fighting near Mandalay, and dashed south to try to reopen the road and railroad. Soon a tremendous battle was raging around Meiktila. For a while the intensity of the Japanese counterattacks completely surrounded the 17th Indian Division.

But Slim had expected this, and so he sent reinforcements by air to join the 17th Division at its captured airfields. The 7th Division also began fighting its way eastward from Pagan to Meiktila.

At the same time, the British who had crossed the Irrawaddy near Mandalay renewed their assaults. Because the Japanese defenses had been weakened when Kimura had sent detachments south to Meiktila, the British soon broke out of their bridgeheads. While the 19th Division fought its way into Mandalay from the north, the others surged southeast toward Meiktila.

Kimura now knew that he was beaten. His only hope lay in smashing or going around the British positions at Meiktila. The battle around that ruined town flared into even greater intensity, but the Japanese could not break through. Now they found themselves being surrounded by the converging British drives from the north and west. Kimura ordered his troops to withdraw east of Meiktila, and then to retreat south.

British riflemen guard the slopes of Mandalay Hill as a battle rages below them.

THE RACE TO RANGOON

Shwebo

Lashio

MANDALAY

Taunggyi

ARAKAN

Akyab

Meiktila
MARCH 4

Magwe

Loikaw

7TH DIV.

20TH DIV.

Salween R.

Bay of Bengal

Prome
MAY 2

Toungoo
APR. 22

Irrawaddy R.

Sittang R.

APR. 29

17TH DIV.

Pegu

Bilin

Paan

5TH & 17TH DIV.

MOULMEIN

0   75

RANGOON
MAY 2-3

Scale of Miles

The Final Operations

Now THE JAPANESE suffered another blow. As their front crumbled in central Burma, the Burma National Army, which the Japanese had trained and equipped, revolted and joined the British. General Aung San, commander of the Burmese troops, had long been in secret contact with the British, and had made careful plans for this revolt. Slipping off into the jungle, the Burmese began to harass the distressed Japanese. Though they played only a small part in the final victory, the Burmese unquestionably helped the British in their race for Rangoon during April, 1945.

And this was really a race — between two rival British corps that wanted each for itself the honor of capturing Rangoon. It was also a race against time, since the monsoon rains were expected to start in a month, at the beginning of May. Once the rains began, the British tanks would be useless, and all large-scale operations would have to stop.

The armored units of the 17th Indian Division spearheaded the drive of the British IV Corps to the southward toward Rangoon. They reached Pegu, just north of Rangoon, on May 1, the day the rains started. That same day the XV Corps, from its captured bases in the Arakan, made an amphibious landing at the mouth of the Irrawaddy River, south of Rangoon. These forces joined each other at the capital of Burma on May 3, 1945. The Japanese had abandoned the city two days earlier as they retreated eastward across the Sittang River, toward Thailand.

For all practical purposes this ended World War II in Burma. Scattered and confused fighting continued as the British cleared the country of isolated Japanese units that had survived their terrible defeats. But because of the monsoon, no large-scale pursuit into Thailand was possible. The British now prepared for an amphibious assault to recapture Singapore when the dry weather began in the fall of 1945. But the war ended before this operation could begin.

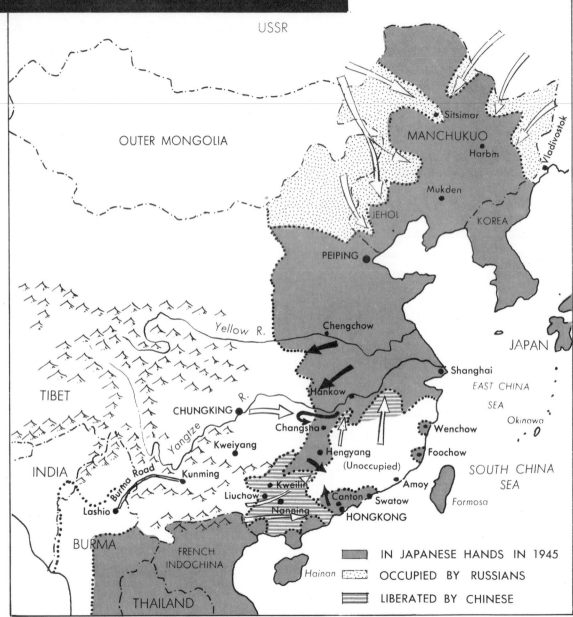

FINAL OPERATIONS IN CHINA

USSR

OUTER MONGOLIA

MANCHUKUO

Sitsimar

Harbin

Vladivostok

JEHOL

Mukden

KOREA

PEIPING

Yellow R.

Chengchow

JAPAN

TIBET

Hankow

Shanghai

EAST CHINA

SEA

Okinawa

CHUNGKING

Yangtze R.

Changsha

Kweiyang

Hengyang

Wenchow

(Unoccupied)

Foochow

INDIA

Kunming

SOUTH CHINA

Burma Road

Kweilin

SEA

Liuchow

Amoy

Lashio

Nanning

Canton

Swatow

Formosa

HONGKONG

BURMA

FRENCH

INDOCHINA

Hainan

IN JAPANESE HANDS IN 1945

OCCUPIED BY RUSSIANS

THAILAND

LIBERATED BY CHINESE

Victory—and a New War—in China

Renewal of the Japanese Offensives

AFTER CHINESE counterattacks had stopped the Japanese advance on Kweiyang in December, 1944, General Wedemeyer began to reorganize the Chinese army and to prepare for counteroffensives that he hoped to start in mid-1945. His excellent plans were much like those that Stilwell had attempted, but Wedemeyer was more diplomatic than "Vinegar Joe," and he soon gained the confidence of Chiang.

Despite their repulse at Kweiyang, the Japanese did not relax their pressure. In late January and early February, 1945, while suppressing widespread Chinese guerrilla activity in the areas they had conquered, they began an offensive to capture the railroad line from Hengyang to Canton. Chinese ground opposition was ineffective. Repeated attacks by the American Fourteenth Air Force were unable to prevent the Japanese from seizing the entire railroad line.

Then, in late March, the Japanese attacked westward on a broad front between the Yellow and Yangtze Rivers, with the objective of capturing American air bases at Laohokow and Ankang. Surprising the Allies, they rapidly approached Laohokow, where they were held up for two weeks by hard-fighting Chinese troops before they captured the town and the airfield on April 8th.

Wedemeyer and Chiang rushed reinforcements to the front. On April 10, the Chinese counterattacked. The Japanese were driven back almost to Laohokao; their offensive was effectively halted.

The Japanese now shifted their attention farther south, attacking westward from Changsha toward Changteh and Chihkiang. Their purpose was to conquer a rich rice-growing area, and also to seize the American air base at Chihkiang.

59

As the Japanese were approaching Changteh on May 8, they were struck by a counterattack. The Chinese assault was spearheaded by the two divisions which had been sent from Burma five months earlier. With excellent support from General Chennault's air force, the Chinese threw the Japanese back with heavy losses to Changsha. This was the first serious defeat the Japanese had experienced in China for more than two years.

Japanese Withdrawal

THE DEFEAT at Changteh, combined with disasters elsewhere on its far-flung fighting fronts, caused Japan to decide to evacuate south China. Burma had been lost; the Allied troops there were now available not only to attack Singapore and Malaya, but also to reinforce the main Chinese armies in China. In the Pacific, the surging American advance had captured Iwo Jima and most of Okinawa.

Also, Germany had just surrendered, which meant that American and British troops — and probably Russian as well — would soon be available for operations in the Far East. There seemed little hope for Japan now, other than to so strengthen her defenses that attacks would become too costly for the Allies. In this way the Japanese government hoped to make a negotiated peace, instead of being forced to unconditional surrender. With this desperate, and almost hopeless strategy in mind, the Japanese began their withdrawal from south China in May.

The Chinese now began to advance against the retreating Japanese, but although they harassed the withdrawing columns, they were unable to interfere seriously with the Japanese troop movements. The greatest losses suffered by the Japanese were from the wide-ranging and efficient attacks of the Fourteenth Air Force.

Considerable fighting continued on the ground, however, as Japanese rear guards stubbornly delayed Chinese pursuit. On July 27, the revived Chinese army recaptured the former American airfield at Kweilin.

The Potsdam Proclamation

ONE DAY EARLIER, American President Harry Truman and British Prime Minister Clement Attlee had issued the Potsdam Proclamation, demanding the unconditional surrender of Japan, but promising a just peace. The Allied leaders threatened, however, that if the Japanese forces did not surrender promptly, Japan would be destroyed.

The Allies later learned that the Japanese tried to respond to this peace offer by a message sent through Russia, which was still neutral in the war in Asia. By this time, however, the Russians had determined to join the war against Japan, in accordance with promises that they had made to their British and American allies earlier in 1945. Since Generalissimo Stalin wanted to make sure that Soviet troops participated in final victory over Japan, he did not want the war to end before he was ready to enter.

But the Americans and British thought that the Japanese had ignored the Potsdam Proclamation, and so they began to carry out their threat to destroy Japan. On August 6, the first atom bomb was dropped on the Japanese city of Hiroshima.

Russian Entry into the War

THE RUSSIANS, realizing that Japan could not long continue to resist, declared war two days later. Three powerful Russian army groups, under the overall command of Marshal Alexander M. Vasilevski, in-

Aboard the U.S.S. *Missouri.* Just as the Japanese were about to be given their copy of the surrender, it was discovered that Canada had signed on the wrong line. Here Lieutenant General Walter Sutherland, Chief of Staff for General MacArthur, corrects the mistake.

vaded Manchuria from the east, north, and west. Japanese troops withdrew in front of the advancing Russian columns, without offering serious opposition.

Japanese Surrender

ON AUGUST 12, Japan again offered to make peace. She sent a message to the Allies through the Swiss government, agreeing to the terms stated in the Potsdam Proclamation. Procedures for the surrender of Japanese troops were quickly arranged, and on August 15 combat operations ended. The official signing of the Japanese surrender took place on the USS *Missouri* in Tokyo Bay on September 2. All Allied forces were represented.

Under the terms of the surrender, Chinese troops were to reoccupy all of the areas of China held by Japan, save for Manchuria. Japanese troops in Manchuria were to surrender to the Russians, who were then supposed to turn the province back to the National Government of China.

In late August and early September the surrender terms were carried out. American troops occupied the islands of Japan. At Singapore, Admiral Lord Louis Mountbatten received the surrender of the Japanese in Southeast Asia. In China, the troops of Chiang Kai-shek liberated occupied China and began sending the Japanese troops back to their islands on American ships. The Russians promptly and efficiently occupied Manchuria, after accepting the Japanese surrender. Korea was occupied by American and Russian troops.

Manchuria — and Civil War

CHIANG KAI-SHEK's forces meanwhile moved north toward Manchuria so as to be able to take over control of the country as the Russians withdrew. But the Russians did not leave.

For several months the Russians remained in Manchuria. Instead of sending the captured troops back to Japan, they evacuated them to Siberia, where they indoctrinated many of them with Communist propaganda. At the same time, the Russians dismantled the large Japanese factories in Manchuria, and sent them back into Russian territory to be reassembled.

During all this time the Russians were quietly letting Mao Tse-tung's Chinese Communists move into Manchuria. Mao's troops were permitted to take over captured Japanese weapons and military equipment. Not until late November did the Russians begin to evacuate Manchuria, and as they withdrew, the Chinese Communists immediately took control.

The long-dormant civil war between the Chinese Communists and Chiank Kai-shek's National Government of China flared once again. The Chinese people, who had suffered horribly during eight years of war, suddenly found that the long-hoped-for peace was non-existent. Manchuria, already a prize and a battleground for four wars in half a century, was the scene of the beginning of a new civil war that would threaten the entire world's peace for many years to come.

Index

65